A World of Sport

Written by Paul Mason
Illustrated by Dave Hill

What is sport?

Sport is an activity. When people play sport, they compete against each other – they try their hardest to play the game well and to win. Most people play sport for fun, but for some it is a job. People have been playing sports for thousands of years.

The ancient Egyptians played many different sports. They played sport for fun and to keep fit and healthy.

They did wrestling, swimming and gymnastics. The pharaohs (or kings) liked to watch sport.

The Olympic Games™

The Olympic Games began in ancient Greece in 776 BC. One of the events was the pentathlon. There were five different sports in the pentathlon event: the long jump, the javelin throw, the discus throw, a running race and a wrestling match.

Another event was chariot racing. Horses pulled chariots driven by charioteers. The fastest charioteer was the winner.

An ancient Greek chariot race

The Olympic Games were very important to the ancient Greeks. Today, over 200 countries compete at the Olympics.

Sport is everywhere

There are team sports like football and individual sports like running. There are ball sports and bat sports. There are sports that need animals and sports that use wheels. Some sports don't need any equipment at all.

Volleyball

Gymnastics

Swimming

Skiing

Sports can be played on the ground, in the water, on the snow and in the air. Can you name one of each of these types of sport?

Sports are played all around the world.

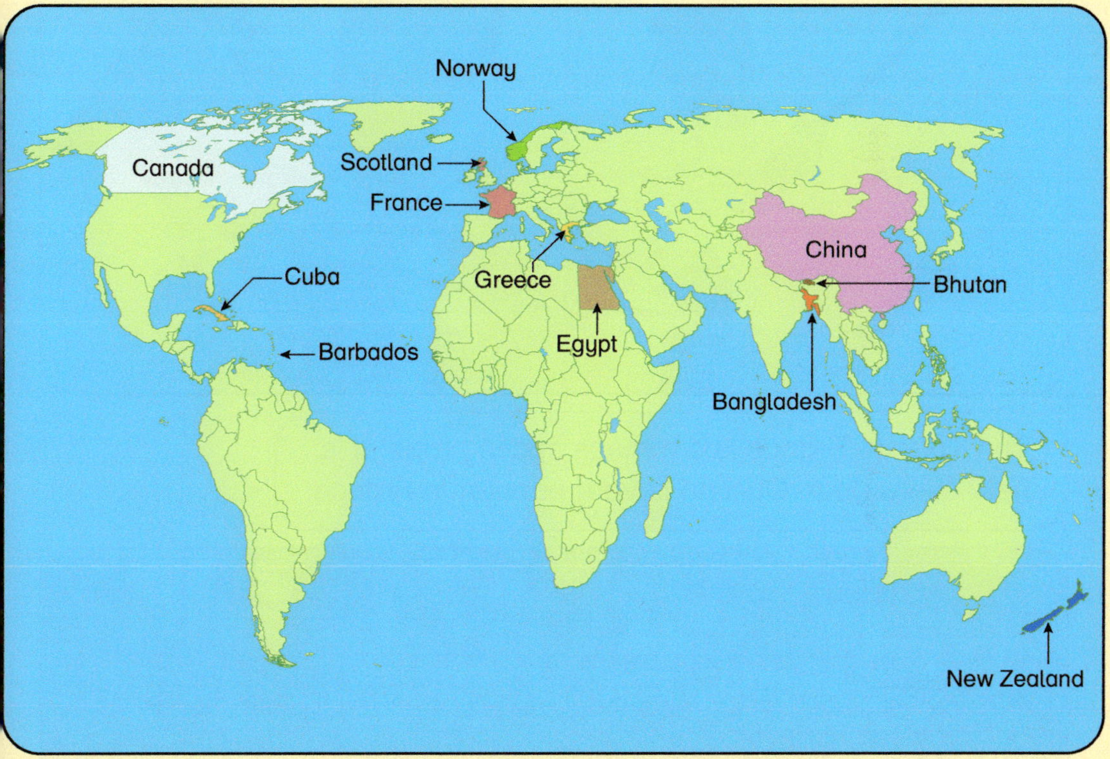

Many countries have a national sport – a sport the country is famous for. It is often the most popular sport in the country. A country's national sport is an important part of its culture and history.

Popular sports

In some countries, the national sport is set by law. In Canada, the law says that the national winter sport is ice hockey.

The Tour de France is a famous cycling race. It is held every year. Cycling is very popular in France.

Let's look at some other popular sports from around the world.

Bangladesh: Kabaddi

In kabaddi, there are two teams. One team is on one side of a small field (or beach), the other team is on the other side.

A player from one team runs to the other side of the field. She is called a raider. She tries to touch someone from the other team.

Then the raider has to get back to her side of the field without getting caught. To make it hard, she must hold her breath. The raider says, 'Kabaddi, kabaddi, kabaddi!'

New Zealand: Rugby

Rugby is the most popular sport in New Zealand.

The national rugby team is called the All Blacks. This is because the players wear black rugby shirts.

Before the All Blacks play a rugby match, they do a *haka*. The *haka* is a type of strong dance. It means that the All Blacks are going to try very hard to win.

Scotland: Golf

Scotland is the home of golf. Golf started in Scotland in the 1400s. It is an important part of the country's history and tradition. Golf is now played all over the world.

Golf players use a golf club to hit the ball. They try to get the ball into the hole. Golf players want to get a 'hole in one'. This means they only hit the ball once and it goes into the hole.

Did you know?
In Japan, if a golf player gets a hole in one, they must have a party for all their friends.

Cuba: Baseball

Baseball arrived in Cuba in the 1860s. Some students from Cuba played it in the United States and then they took the game home to Cuba. Baseball quickly became very popular.

Today baseball is part of everyday life in Cuba. There are many teams all over the country. One of the most famous teams is the Industriales, from the city of Havana. Their nickname is Los Leones – 'the lions'.

Barbados: Cricket

On the island of Barbados, the team sport of cricket is very popular. It is played all over the island – on village streets, on the beach and in large cricket grounds. It is played all year.

When the people of Barbados are not playing cricket, they are watching it! The cricket grounds in Barbados are always full of people watching the game. People also watch it on TV.

Bhutan: Archery

Archery is a sport that uses a bow and arrow. The archer pulls back the bow string. Then he fires the arrow and tries to hit a target far away. He tries to get the arrow right in the middle of the target.

In the past in Bhutan, many people used a bow and arrow for hunting. Now archery is the national sport of Bhutan.

The archer pulls back the bow string.

The arrows hit the target.

Archery competitions take place all over Bhutan. People watch and cheer loudly for their favourite player.

Norway: Cross-country skiing

Cross-country skiing is a winter sport. People have been skiing in Norway for thousands of years. At first, skiing was a way to travel over the snow. Today, many people in Norway ski for fun. Children in Norway learn to ski when they are very young.

Did you know?

In 1911, skiing helped an explorer from Norway to be the first person to reach the South Pole. Roald Amundsen used skis to travel over the snow.

Being a good sport

It is important to be a 'good sport'. A good sport tries their best and plays by the rules. It doesn't matter if they win or lose – good sports treat the other players fairly.

People from all around the world like playing sport. Do you like sport? What do you play? What is your country's national sport?

Snow Rescue

Written by Paul Mason

Illustrated by Dave Hill

The school bus raced along the road through the forest. On board, the children were excited. They were going on a school sports trip. There were going to be lots of sports – archery, cycling, football and even swimming in the lake! Jade, Samantha, Mike and Jack couldn't wait to get there.
I can't wait to get to the cabin!
Me too!
We can explore the forest.
A whole weekend of sports!
But one student wasn't excited – Anders, the exchange student from Norway. He was far away from home and he was very lonely.

Finally, they arrived! The cabin was in the middle of the forest, a long way from the nearest town. Everyone in the class got off the bus and looked around. It was beautiful.
OK, class. Get your bags off the bus and find your rooms.
Yes, Mr Fleming.

But Mrs Harvey and Miss Olive were worried.
I think those dark clouds are coming our way.
They could bring snow.

Mr Fleming opened the door to the old cabin and the children raced to choose their beds. Anders walked slowly on his own. He didn't really want to be on the trip.
I get the top bed!
Not if I get there first!

Miss Olive and Mrs Harvey found their room. Mrs Harvey was starting to feel ill.
Are you feeling OK, Mrs Harvey? You look pale.
I'll be fine. I'll just lie down for a bit.

That night, as the children sat around the log fire, the snow began to fall. It fell slowly at first, then faster and faster.
Snow!
But what about the football game in the morning?
We can have a snowball fight instead!
Count me in!

But Mrs Harvey couldn't stop shivering. She went to bed early.

The next morning, there was snow all around the cabin. The children dug out a path. The road was under the snow, too. The children couldn't play football, but they were very excited.

But the teachers were getting worried. Mrs Harvey was not well. She did not get up for breakfast – she stayed in bed. Mr Fleming tried to phone the doctor, but the phone in the cabin didn't work.

But Anders had an idea. He knew there were some skis in the cabin. Back home in Norway he used skis every winter. Skiing was the national sport. Anders learnt to ski when he was very young. Maybe they could ski to the town!
Mr Fleming! What about the skis? We can use them to get help.
But I can't ski.
I can ski a bit. Anders and I can go, and he can help me.

Anders and Mr Fleming took the skis off the wall and took them outside. The children watched while Anders helped Miss Olive put them on.

Anders led the way through the thick snow. Miss Olive waved goodbye to Mr Fleming and the children.

The road through the forest was thick with snow. Their skis swished over the snow. It made Anders remember the cross-country skiing races in Norway. Miss Olive was doing her best to keep up.
You're doing very well, Miss Olive.
This is hard work. I'm glad we're fit and healthy.

Soon they could see the town in the distance. They started to go faster.
It's not far now.
I hope Mrs Harvey is OK.

Back at the cabin, the children were worried. Anders and Miss Olive had been gone for a long time.
Do you think they're OK?
I'm sure they're fine.
Anders knows what he's doing.

Mr Fleming was worried about Mrs Harvey.
Oh dear. She's getting worse.

Just then, a rumbling noise came from the forest. The noise got closer and closer. Jade and Mike went outside to see what it was.
What's that noise?
It sounds like an engine.

Suddenly a snowplough came through the trees. It was clearing the blocked road. Anders and Miss Olive were in the snowplough with the driver! And with them was the doctor.
It's them!
They made it!
Thank goodness.

Later, after seeing the doctor and taking some medicine, Mrs Harvey was much better. Everyone sat in front of the fire, drinking hot chocolate. The children wanted to hear all about the snow rescue. Everyone wanted to talk to Anders. What a good sport he was! Now Anders had a big smile on his face. He was happy he was on the sports trip.

Activities

1 Complete the sentences.

national ~~thousands~~ world healthy football Games

1 People have been playing sports for thousands of years.

2 The ancient Egyptians played sports to keep fit and ________ .

3 The Olympic ________ began in Greece in 776 BC.

4 There are team sports like ________ .

5 Sports are played around the ________ .

6 Many countries have a ________ sport.

2 Circle T (True) or F (False).

1	Kabaddi is the national sport of France.	T	(F)
2	The New Zealand rugby team is called the All Blacks.	T	F
3	Golf began in Scotland in the 1400s.	T	F
4	Baseball was brought to Cuba from Bhutan.	T	F
5	Cricket is not popular in Barbados.	T	F
6	Archers use bows and arrows.	T	F
7	Skiing helped a man from Norway to be the first person to reach the South Pole.	T	F

3 Read the story. Then match 1–7 with a–g.

1 The school bus raced along
2 Anders was far away from home
3 The cabin was in the middle of the forest,
4 The children couldn't play football,
5 Anders learnt to ski
6 Miss Olive waved goodbye
7 The road through the forest

a when he was very young.
b was thick with snow.
c the road through the forest.
d but they were very excited.
e and he felt very lonely.
f to Mr Fleming and the children.
g a long way from the nearest town.

4 Write the words.

Down

1 

2 

3 

4 

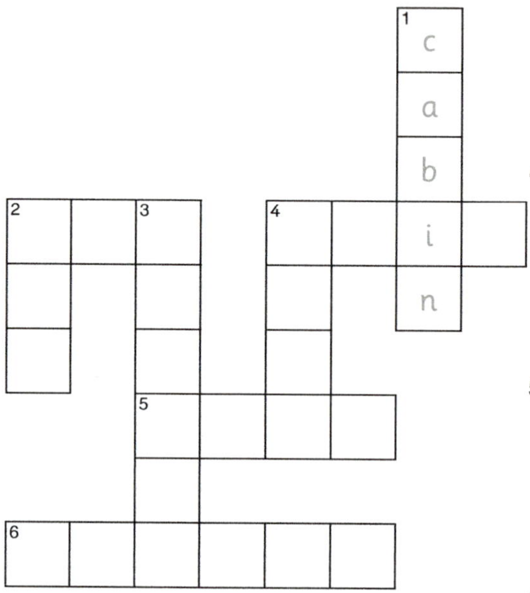

Across

2 

4 

5 

6 

5 Who said what?

1 OK, class. Get your bags off the bus and find your rooms.

2 I think those dark clouds are coming our way.

3 Are you feeling OK, Mrs Harvey? You look pale.

4 What about the skis? We can use them to get help.

a 

b 

c 

d 

6 Put the sentences in order.

[ ] A snowplough came through the trees.

[ ] Anders had an idea.

[1] Everyone in the class got off the bus and looked around. It was beautiful.

[ ] Mrs Harvey couldn't stop shivering. She went to bed early.

[ ] Anders led the way through the thick snow.

[ ] Just then, a rumbling noise came from the forest.

[ ] Soon they could see the town in the distance.

7 Find the eight sports words.

D	Y	W	R	E	S	T	L	I	N	G	G
G	Q	S	R	L	B	Y	P	S	R	Y	U
G	U	R	X	L	B	K	L	U	J	M	W
O	J	U	Q	S	W	I	M	M	I	N	G
L	F	T	W	R	M	I	G	G	W	A	Q
F	F	O	O	T	B	A	L	L	P	S	U
P	A	F	H	D	H	B	O	H	Q	T	T
T	H	H	O	C	K	E	Y	F	D	I	B
X	E	R	U	I	W	N	X	V	W	C	E
A	S	P	O	R	T	A	N	G	N	S	L
V	S	K	O	G	T	T	A	A	Y	P	P
L	M	E	D	B	A	S	E	B	A	L	L

8 What is your favourite sport? Why? Write and draw.

My favourite sport is football.
I like playing with my friends.

Bilingual Dictionary

Key: (n) = noun (v) = verb (adj) = adjective (adv) = adverb

Write the words in your language.

activity (n) ____________
adventure (n) ____________
ancient (adj) ____________
archery (n) ____________
baseball (n) ____________
bat (n) ____________
blocked (adj) ____________
cabin (n) ____________
chariot (n) ____________
compete (v) ____________
competition (n) ____________
cross-country skiing (n) ____________
culture (n) ____________
cycling (n) ____________
discus (n) ____________
early (adj) ____________
equipment (n) ____________
event (n) ____________
exchange (n) ____________
excited (adj) ____________
explore (v) ____________
fairly (adv) ____________
famous (adj) ____________
fit (adj) ____________
gymnastics (n) ____________
healthy (adj) ____________
history (n) ____________
hunting (n) ____________
ice hockey (n) ____________

important (adj) ____________
individual (adj) ____________
javelin (n) ____________
lonely (adj) ____________
lose (v) ____________
national (adj) ____________
pentathlon (n) ____________
phone (n) ____________
play (v) ____________
popular (adj) ____________
race (v) ____________
raider (n) ____________
rescue (n) ____________
rugby (n) ____________
safety (n) ____________
scared (adj) ____________
shiver (v) ____________
ski (n, v) ____________
snow (n) ____________
snowplough (n) ____________
sport (n) ____________
strong (adj) ____________
swimming (n) ____________
swished (v) ____________
target (n) ____________
team (n) ____________
travel (v) ____________
trip (n) ____________
win (v) ____________
wrestling (n) ____________

Macmillan Education
4 Crinan Street
London N1 9XW
A division of Springer Nature Limited
Companies and representatives throughout the world

ISBN 978-1-3800-4192-0

Written by Paul Mason

First published 2014
This edition published 2019

Designed by Carolyn Gibson
Illustrated by Peter Harper (p5) and Dave Hill
Picture research by Victoria Gaunt
Cover photograph by Imagesource

The author and publishers would like to thank the following for permission to reproduce their photographs: **Alamy Stock Photo**/: Science History Images p3, Alamy Stock Photo/ Oliver Förstner p6(b), Alamy/Greg Balfour Evans p9, Alamy/Keren Su/China Span p12(b), Alamy/View Stock p2(t); **Bridgeman Art Library**/Courtesy of Swann Auction Galleries p13(b); **Getty Images**/Richard Newstead p1, Getty Images/Daniel Milchev p4(br), Getty Images/rayna p4(bl), Getty Images pp7, 8(t, b), Getty Images/AFP pp10, 13(t), Getty Images/Hero Images p14(bl), Getty Images/iStock/aabejon p14(tr), Getty Images/Peter Adams p12(t), Getty Images/Upperhall Ltd/Robert Harding p2(b), Getty Images/Tim Macpherson p14(br); **Glow Images**/Benis Arapovic p4(tl); **Image Source**/Christopher Robbins p4(tr), Imagesource p14(tl); **JJ pixs** / Alamy Stock Photo p11; **Photoshot**/Tips p6(t).

Printed and bound in Brazil

2025
14